THE JOURNEY TO A PERFECT WEDDING

Aderonke Samuel

COPYRIGHT

Copyright © 2025 by Aderonke Samuel

All rights reserved. No part of this publication may be reproduced, stored in a retrieval system, or transmitted in any form or by any means—electronic, mechanical, photocopying, recording, or otherwise—without the prior written permission of the publisher, except in the case of brief quotations embodied in critical articles or reviews.

Published in the United States by

GAIN Publishing LLC

Canal Winchester, OH

ISBN: 979-8-9987965-1-7

Cover Design by: Nneoma Anointing Sambo

Interior Design by: Muna Fausta

Printed in the United States

Unless otherwise indicated, all Scripture quotations are taken from the King James Version (KJV) of the Bible, which is in the public domain.

This is a work of nonfiction. Any resemblance to real persons, living or dead, is purely coincidental unless explicitly stated by the author.

DISCLAIMER:

This book is intended for informational and inspirational purposes only. It is not a substitute for professional counseling, legal, medical, or psychological advice. Readers are encouraged to seek appropriate professional guidance for their specific circumstances. The author and publisher disclaim any liability for any outcomes that may result from the application of information contained in this book.

For rights and permissions, contact:

info@gospelaffairs.com

Aderonke Samuel

DEDICATION

This book is humbly dedicated to the Author of Marriage, the God of Heaven and Earth!

Aderonke Samuel

ACKNOWLEDGEMENTS

I have always desired to write—not just one book, but many—that will help people build strong and fulfilling relationships and marriages. I am deeply grateful to God for allowing me to bring this vision to life.

Many people contributed to making this book a reality, and I sincerely appreciate each of them.

I am especially grateful to my husband, Dr. Noah Samuel, who, alongside our children, provided the encouragement and supportive environment I needed to complete this book. His unwavering support and love were instrumental in its creation. He is a true example of a godly man, not just for allowing me to pursue my God-ordained purpose but actively helping me soar. Marriage with him has been a beautiful and fulfilling journey.

I am also thankful for the wonderful children God has blessed us with—Toluwanimi and Enioluwafe—who are incredibly loving and caring. They were my greatest encouragers, inspiring me to take the step to write this book.

A special appreciation goes to Pastor Bisi Adewale, whose mentorship and strategic guidance illuminated the path for me. Attending his book-writing training, *The Millionaire Authors' Boot Camp*, gave me the push to take a leap of faith and bring this book to life.

Aderonke Samuel

To everyone who played a role in this journey—thank you. Your support and encouragement mean the world to me.

Aderonke Samuel

FOREWORD

Marriage is more than a ceremony. It's a covenant, a lifelong journey of love, growth, and purpose. In The Journey To A Perfect Wedding, Aderonke Samuel masterfully bridges the gap between the dream of a flawless wedding day and the reality of building a resilient, joyfilled marriage.

Drawing from her rich experience as a relationship coach and her own heartfelt journey, Aderonke offers more than advice; she provides a roadmap. With biblical wisdom woven into practical guidance, this book addresses the critical questions many couples overlook: How do you choose a partner aligned with your purpose? What role does faith play in sustaining love? How can you avoid the pitfalls of unrealistic expectations?

Through candid stories—like the groom's outburst over a misplaced meal or her own lessons from wedding-day mishaps—Aderonke underscores the importance of intentionality, communication, and spiritual grounding. Her insights on balancing cultural traditions, financial prudence, and emotional preparedness are both refreshing and revolutionary.

Whether you're single, engaged, or seeking to strengthen your marriage, this book is a treasure. It challenges readers to look beyond

Aderonke Samuel

the allure of a "perfect wedding" and invest in what truly lasts: a union rooted in God, mutual respect, and unwavering commitment.

Aderonke's voice is both compassionate and authoritative, making this guide not just informative but transformative. Let her journey inspire yours as you step into a marriage that reflects grace, purpose, and enduring love.

PASTOR BISI ADEWALE

International Family Coach

Author of more than 130 books on relationships, marriage, parenting and total family life.

TABLE OF CONTENTS

DEDICATION

ACKNOWLEDGEMENTS

FOREWORD

INTRODUCTION _____ 10

CHAPTER ONE:

SEEKING GOD'S GUIDANCE _____ 15

CHAPTER TWO:

YOUR MARRIAGE AND PURPOSE _____ 21

CHAPTER THREE:

BE INTENTIONAL ABOUT FRIENDSHIP _____ 33

CHAPTER FOUR:

TALK ABOUT YOUR FUTURE _____ 39

CHAPTER FIVE:

MENTAL BELIEFS _____ 47

CHAPTER SIX:

INTENTIONALITY AND DETERMINATION _____ 60

CHAPTER SEVEN:

EXPECTATIONS IN MARRIAGE _____ 65

CHAPTER EIGHT:

PLANS BEFORE PICKING A WEDDING DATE _____ 77

CHAPTER NINE:

THE WEDDING DAY _____ 89

CHAPTER TEN:

DON'T STOP LEARNING _____ 94

OUR STORY_____ 97

INTRODUCTION

A wedding day is a very special occasion in the life of an engaged couple—a day that many dream of. It is a day of celebration, marking the official union of two lovers who vow to spend their lives together in holy matrimony. It is the beginning of a new home. On this significant day, vows are exchanged, and lifelong commitments are made.

Some people fantasize for years about how their wedding day will be. And yes, I understand—it should be glamorous. After all, it is a day to be remembered for good, not just for the couple but for their families, too. It is one of those rare occasions when all attention is focused on the bride and groom. It is also a day when two lovers can freely express their affection, even sharing a kiss in the presence of their parents without hesitation or restriction.

A wedding day is more than just a celebration; it marks the beginning of reality in marriage. It is the day when a couple embarks on a journey of truly getting to know each other beyond the romance of courtship. Many events unfold in just this one day. It is also a time when extended families from both sides come together, sometimes meeting formally for the first time. If well planned, it is a joyous occasion for the newlyweds and their loved ones.

Furthermore, a wedding day holds spiritual significance. The Bible, in Matthew 19:5, states that a man should leave his parents and be fully united with his wife, becoming one with her. At this point, responsibility shifts, as the couple must build their life together, independent of their parents' support. It is the day a man is officially called a husband and a woman, a wife.

WHAT A WEDDING DAY SHOULD NOT BE

A wedding day should not be the last time a couple feels the butterflies of love before their passion begins to fade. It should not be the last day they express affection or excitement for each other. Unfortunately, this is the reality for some couples—I have witnessed marriages where the spark began to die right after the wedding.

A wedding day should not be the last time couples go on dates or invest in their relationship. Though it is a joyful occasion for most, it can also be a day of conflict. I have attended weddings where, rather than bringing families together, the event created lasting rifts between extended relatives. A wedding should never be a day that breeds enmity—it should remain a day of love and happiness.

I want to share a true-life story to illustrate how an engagement ceremony, which is supposed to be a joyous event, can turn into a day of sorrow and even lead to a troubled marriage.

A WEDDING THAT TURNED SOUR

I once attended an engagement ceremony that nearly fell apart due to the poor handling of a seemingly small situation. The main issue arose from how one of the food servers at the bride's house treated the groom's father.

In many African cultures, the groom's family visits the bride's family to formally request her hand in marriage during the introduction and engagement ceremony. Some couples hold both ceremonies on the same day to save costs, while others separate them. Some even conduct the engagement ceremony a day before the white wedding—though not all couples opt for a white wedding, as it is considered a Western tradition. The decision ultimately depends on the couple's preference and agreement.

In this particular case, the couple chose to have their engagement the day before their church wedding. Ideally, nothing should go wrong the day before a wedding, but unfortunately, that was not the case.

At the engagement, the groom was smiling as his bride was brought in to sit beside him. However, after a while, his demeanor changed for reasons known only to him. Soon after the bride's entrance, the food servers began distributing meals to guests. One of them unknowingly gave a plate of food to the groom's father, only to take it back and hand it to someone else.

The server did not recognize the groom's father, but the groom noticed everything from where he was sitting. After some time, when he still did not see his father eating while others around him were served, he could no longer hold back his emotions. Suddenly, he burst out in anger, shouting, *"Why won't you serve my father?"* His voice was loud enough for everyone to hear.

The bride, sitting beside him, tried to calm him down, but at that point, he had already lost control. As more people attempted to pacify him, he grew even angrier and ended up insulting his father-in-law, who had also been trying to defuse the situation. He did not care that guests were watching. One statement he made remains in my memory: *"I am not interested anymore! How can they disrespect my father like this over food?"* He was crying and shouting as he said this.

The embarrassment was overwhelming. The bride, unable to withstand the humiliation, left the gathering in tears, saying, *"This is supposed to be my happy day—what is happening?"* That single incident drastically altered the relationship between both families.

Sadly, as I write this, the couple has since separated. I still remember hearing guests at the event predicting that their marriage would not last—and it didn't. The situation that unfolded at their engagement was just the beginning of deeper issues in their relationship.

LESSONS TO LEARN

It is clear from the story that the groom was not the only one at fault. Though he failed to control his emotions, the situation could have been avoided with better planning. Proper measures should have been in place to ensure that such conflicts did not arise.

So why am I sharing this? To emphasize that a wedding day is about much more than setting a date, dressing beautifully, and exchanging vows. It is a sensitive occasion that requires careful preparation. Before the wedding, couples should consider important factors such as:

- Whom they are marrying
- The structure of the day's events
- Who is responsible for what?

In the following pages, I will discuss these critical measures to help ensure that your wedding day remains joyful and memorable.

1

SEEKING GOD'S GUIDANCE

"House and wealth are inherited from fathers, but a prudent wife is from the Lord."

- Proverbs 19:14

The power of prayer in choosing a life partner cannot be overemphasized. When God sees that you are genuinely seeking His guidance, He will redirect your path if you are heading in the wrong direction. Seeking Him means entrusting both your present and future into His hands.

If you want to be sure that the person you are with is truly right for you, seeking God's guidance is essential. The reason for this is not only to involve Him in your journey but also to allow Him to guide your decision-making. God can reveal potential issues that might arise in the future—things you may not have noticed. He is capable of doing all things, including giving you peace of mind regarding your choice of a partner, but He wants you to ask. As stated in Matthew 7:7, *"Ask, and it will be given to you; seek, and you will find; knock, and the door will be opened to you"*.

Some people say that God reveals their spouse to them through dreams or other signs, while others experience an overwhelming sense of peace as confirmation from Him. The way God communicates with you about who to marry depends on your relationship with Him. This is why it is important to cultivate a relationship with God before you reach the stage of choosing a life partner. Do not seek Him only when you need direction—build a connection with Him long before that time comes.

My confirmation about my husband came through the peace of mind I felt. God did not show me a vision, but I noticed something significant. Before I met my husband, I always desired a peaceful, loving, and beautiful marriage. Though I did not know how it would happen, I consistently prayed about my future home. I take my prayers seriously, and at the time, most of my prayers revolved around marriage and my relationship with my future mother-in-law.

In my previous relationships, my constant prayer was, *"God, if this person is not meant for me or will not bring me peace, let the relationship end, even without any possibility of restoration"*. And I must confess—this is exactly what happened.

However, when I met my husband, my prayers changed. I no longer asked God to end the relationship if it wasn't meant to be; instead, my prayer became, *"God, bless the home we will build together"*. This shift in prayer was because I had complete peace in my heart—I no longer felt the need to pray for God to remove him from my life.

Ordinarily, my relationship with my husband should not have led to marriage because we came from different religious backgrounds. Although I was born into a Christian family through my father, I was raised by my mother's family, who were Muslims. In the past, I had turned down Christian admirers, telling them that I couldn't date them because of their faith. Yet, here I am, married to a Christian.

This decision is one I will forever be grateful for because it changed my life.

I share this story to emphasize that, despite the religious differences, I had peace of mind. I believe my prayers were answered. But remember—I did not start praying only when I needed a husband. I started praying while I was still in high school. Even though I sought God early, I still made decisions based on my understanding. However, when the time was right, God redirected my plans.

Note that I converted to Christianity two years before our marriage after becoming fully convinced to let go of my previous faith.

So, have you truly sought God's guidance regarding this person? Or is your decision based solely on your feelings and intuition?

Remember, prayers about marriage or choosing a spouse should not begin only when you are ready to get married. They should have started long before that.

CHOOSING A PARTNER

This section of the book is aimed at guiding single women who are in the process of choosing a life partner. I am specifically addressing women in this section because, ultimately, they are the ones who make the decision about whom they want to be with. It is common for a man to express interest in a woman, but it is the woman who decides whether or not to accept that interest. Therefore, the decision of whom to marry largely rests with women, which is why it is crucial for a woman to choose wisely.

Every outcome we experience today is the result of decisions we've made. Marriage is a lifelong commitment that demands thoughtful consideration, yet many people do not fully understand its weight. It is disheartening to see individuals enter into engagements based on reasons that lack depth or substance.

I understand that it may not always be possible to find a partner who possesses every quality you desire, but have you at least ensured that they have the qualities that truly matter to you? I ask this because many people choose their partners for the wrong reasons. In all honesty, we must acknowledge the seriousness of this decision. Some people unintentionally devalue themselves by selecting a partner based on superficial reasons such as:

- Physical beauty.
- Loneliness.
- The desire to have children.
- Societal pressure to get married.
- Wanting to be part of a certain social status.
- Fear of growing old alone.

While these reasons may seem valid on the surface, they should not be the primary motivation for choosing a life partner. The focus should shift towards qualities that truly sustain a lifelong relationship—qualities such as:

- Character.
- Compatibility.

- Shared values.
- Mutual respect.

These are the elements that form the foundation of a meaningful and lasting marriage.

In conclusion, the decision to marry should be grounded in a deep understanding of your partner's character and values, rather than superficial factors. By taking a thoughtful approach, single women can set the stage for fulfilling, enduring marriages that withstand the test of time.

Having evaluated the important qualities, can you confidently say that this person is truly the one for you?

Another important question to ask yourself is, **is this person my friend?**

This question is often overlooked, yet it is crucial. In chapter three, we will explore the benefits of marrying a friend and clarify what marrying your friend truly means.

2

YOUR MARRIAGE AND PURPOSE

"Two are better than one, because they have a good reward for their toil. For if they fall, one will lift up his fellow. But woe to him who is alone when he falls and has not another to lift him up! Again, if two lie together, they keep warm, but how can one keep warm alone? And though a man might prevail against one who is alone, two will withstand him—a threefold cord is not quickly broken."

- Ecclesiastes 4:9-12

Before planning a wedding, have you taken the time to evaluate what you truly know about marriage? I believe it is essential to understand why marriage was created, who created it, and how it is meant to function—especially if you desire to see great results. The reason for this is simple: the wedding day you are eagerly preparing for is just a one-day event, while marriage is a lifetime commitment. To ensure that your wedding day does not become a moment of regret in the future, you need to understand and prepare your mind ahead of time.

Dr. Myles Munroe once said, *"When the purpose of a thing is not known, abuse is inevitable"*. This statement is true for marriage. Many people live as they please or make impulsive decisions simply because they do not understand the purpose of marriage. But surely, you do not want to enter into something you are clueless about just because you believe you are of age or because society tells you it is the right thing to do.

WHAT IS MARRIAGE?

Generally, marriage is a socially and legally binding relationship between a man and a woman, often established to build a family.

THE PURPOSE OF MARRIAGE

The first thing I want to emphasize is that God is the creator of marriage; we can also refer to Him as the designer or manufacturer of marriage. Some people believe that marriage exists solely for procreation, which is the reason many choose to get married in the first place. Some marry simply because they feel the need to have children, without truly embracing the full meaning of marriage or its intended purpose.

While procreation is indeed a reason for marriage, it is not the only reason. There are several purposes behind God's creation of marriage.

1. Companionship

The first purpose of marriage is companionship. When God created Adam, He said, *"It is not good for man to be alone",* which is why He created Eve. God knows we cannot thrive or flourish in isolation—we need one another.

Some people, based on their experiences, may feel they do not need others. However, you must recognize that needing people in your life does not mean you need everyone. Not everyone deserves a place in your life. Some people bring joy, while others drain it. Therefore, be careful about whom you allow into your life.

2. Procreation

Another purpose of marriage is procreation, which is one of the most common reasons people get married. God desires that we populate His kingdom by raising godly children—children who will bring glory to Him.

It has never been God's intention for children to be raised by a single parent. His design for the family is a loving home consisting of both a father and a mother.

I was raised by a single parent, and I must tell you—it was not an easy experience. I am certain that no child desires to grow up in such circumstances, as it can be emotionally and psychologically challenging. This is why it is crucial to choose your spouse wisely, with God's guidance, to ensure that your children do not have to endure the same struggles. I understand that certain situations beyond your control can lead to single parenthood, but I am referring to cases that result from your choices.

Do not marry someone based solely on your current emotions—feelings can be misleading. Take the time to ask yourself the necessary questions before saying, *"I do"*. Remember, if you make the right decision about who becomes the father or mother of your children, they will thank you for it.

3. Reflecting God's Image

The final purpose of marriage that I will mention is that it is meant to represent and reflect God's image.

God is love, and everything He created is beautiful. It is His desire for your marriage to reflect that beauty. A godly marriage brings Him glory, and He is joyful seeing marriages that honor His name.

PRINCIPLES OF MARRIAGE

Did you know there is a manual for marriage? Yes—just like any product created by a manufacturer. When you choose not to follow the instructions or manual that comes with a product, you often encounter difficulties. The same principle applies to marriage. To experience a fulfilling and successful marriage, you need to follow the manual provided by its Creator—God. His guidance is written in *Ephesians 5* in the Bible. All you need to do is read, understand, and apply the teachings from that chapter.

One reason many people struggle in marriage is because they believe they can approach it however they like, relying solely on their understanding.

- **Men, Love Your Wives**

Ephesians 5:25 instructs men to love their wives. This does not mean your wife will always do what you like or expect. God gave this command because He knows that wise women thrive and give their best when they feel genuinely loved by their husbands. A woman who is secure in her husband's love is often willing to go the extra mile to make him happy.

Ask yourself: *Is she the kind of woman I can love unconditionally, as instructed by the marriage manual?* Remember, she won't always meet all your expectations or agree with everything you say.

- **Women, Respect Your Husbands**

Ephesians 5:33 instructs women to respect their husbands. This command does not come with conditions—it does not say to respect him only when he acts respectfully or when you feel he deserves it. Men generally thrive when they feel respected.

One common mistake some women make is withholding respect when their husbands fail to meet their expectations. However, this mindset contradicts the manual provided by the Creator of marriage. In many cases, when a man feels respected—especially when he knows he's falling short—it encourages him to become humbler and considerate.

So, ask yourself: *Will I always respect and honor the person I plan to marry as the head of our family, regardless of his Behaviour?*

Have You Consulted the Manual?

Now that you know a manual exists, have you taken the time to study it and understand what is expected of you? If you focus solely on planning the wedding rather than preparing for the marriage itself, disappointment is almost inevitable. This is why it is crucial not to focus only on the wedding day, the dress, the suit, or the ceremony.

My prayer is that you never look back on your wedding day with regret.

KNOW YOUR PURPOSE

It is also important to understand why you were created. Many people enter marriage without a clear sense of purpose. If you do not know your purpose, you might mistakenly think that you exist solely to get married, but that was never God's intention.

Reflect on these principles and prepare not just for a wedding day but for a lifetime of purposeful and joyful marriage.

Let me share a funny story about myself. When I was in college, there was a time I thought it would have been better if God had made me a leaf—one that would simply fall off the tree as early as possible. I guess this was because I hadn't yet found meaning in life.

There was also a time when I believed my sole purpose in life was to get married. I loved the idea of marriage so much that my only plan was to marry a good man, be a good wife, and have a beautiful family, and that would be it.

Thankfully, I married my lucky charm—the one specially made for me, the person my heart beats for every day. But guess what? After some time, I realized that life is more than just getting married or having a good home. There was an emptiness inside me that led me to seek God in prayer for direction. That was when I discovered my calling in the marriage ministry. Now, I know better, and I desire to live a long and impactful life, touching as many lives as possible.

If you don't want to be in the same uncertain state I was in years ago, I encourage you to seek your Maker and ask why He created you. There is a purpose behind your existence. It is important to understand this even before you get married.

Knowing your purpose will help guide all your decisions, including choosing the right person to marry. When you know why you were created, you will be more careful about who you allow into your life. This understanding will help you focus on what truly matters before entering into any relationship.

So, be mindful of who you allow into your space because marriage goes beyond your present emotions. Do not get into a relationship simply because you're the only one among your friends who is still single or because of desperation. Think about your future, and let this awareness shape your choice of a partner.

Do you realize that your relationship can influence what you become in life? It can also determine how fulfilled you will be. For instance, if you marry someone who has not yet discovered their purpose or does not understand the reason for their existence, they may struggle to help you discover yours.

This could make it difficult for you to fully step into your purpose. After all, people cannot give what they do not have. Someone who has not found meaning in their life may not see the importance of you finding yours. They may struggle to encourage you, especially during the stage when you are still figuring things out for yourself.

This is why it is crucial to be careful about whom you marry. Some people are *purpose killers*, while others are *purpose enhancers*. Purpose killers will frustrate your dreams and make you feel guilty for wanting to pursue your purpose. They won't understand why you seek fulfillment when they have none. Be cautious of such people.

On the other hand, *purpose enhancers* or *helpers* will support you in discovering and fulfilling your purpose—even if you haven't yet figured it out. Your fulfillment in life will always be their priority. Some purpose helpers will go the extra mile, not only allowing you to soar but also helping you take flight once you've found your reason for existence.

A PERSONAL EXPERIENCE

Before I met my husband, I was in a relationship with an insecure man. I realized this when I told him that my mom wanted me to pursue a master's degree. We had both completed our first degree at the same university and were job-hunting at the time.

When I mentioned that my mom had suggested I pursue a master's degree to improve my chances of securing a job, his immediate response was that it wasn't a wise decision. He questioned where my mom would get the money to sponsor me, considering how she had struggled to put me through my first degree.

At first, I thought he was simply concerned about my well-being and didn't want me to suffer. So, I told my mom that I wouldn't be pursuing the program due to our financial situation, especially since she would be the one funding it. But my mom insisted, reassuring me that I shouldn't worry about her—that God would provide. She reminded me that I had always been a considerate child who would manage whatever resources were available without making things difficult for her.

I called my boyfriend to tell him what my mom had said, but he continued to discourage me in every way possible. However, my mom, being a strong African woman, didn't entertain my excuses. So, despite my reservations, I eventually applied for the program.

Before the semester began, I saw a post from my boyfriend on Facebook. He had asked for people's opinions while advising, *"Never allow your woman to rise above you in life. If she becomes more educated than you, she will eventually become proud"*.

Mind you, I hadn't even started the program yet! That was when I realized his objection had never been about financial concerns—it was about his insecurity. But guess what? Despite this clear red flag, I still didn't walk away. I was afraid of starting over. Well, that's a story for another time.

The Lesson?

Choose Wisely.

Your future is just as important as your present. Many people have gone to the grave without fulfilling their purpose—sometimes because of the relationships they were involved in.

Also, remember that having a lot of money does not necessarily mean you will feel fulfilled. Some wealthy people still struggle with feelings of emptiness.

So, choose wisely. Marry someone who will support your growth, not someone who will hinder you. If you live outside of God's purpose for your life, frustration is inevitable. Marriage should never dim your light—it should make your glory shine even brighter. The Bible says, *"One will chase a thousand, but two shall chase ten thousand"*.

Marriage should be an advantage, not a limitation. The Bible also says, *"Two are better than one"*. Couples should help each other fulfil their God-given purposes. If you haven't yet discovered your purpose while single, marriage should help you uncover it—but only if you marry the right person.

A FINAL QUESTION FOR YOU

Before you walk down the aisle, ask yourself: **Will this person allow my light to shine, or will they dim it?**

Here is an important lesson you need to learn: balancing your purpose with your marriage. It would be unwise to focus solely on your purpose while neglecting your marriage. This is one of the reasons some partners may resist their spouse's pursuit of purpose, especially when they feel the other does not know how to maintain a balance between marriage and personal goals.

The question is, have you mastered or are you preparing to master the skill of balancing your purpose with your marriage in a way that one does not negatively impact the other?

3

BE INTENTIONAL ABOUT FRIENDSHIP

"It is better to live in a corner of the housetop than in a house shared with a quarrelsome wife."

- Proverbs 21:9

This chapter highlights the importance and benefits of marrying your friend. I believe this is not the first time you have heard the phrase *"marry your friend"*. I am referring to a genuine, supportive friendship where both partners always have each other's backs. It means being with someone who would never intentionally hurt you.

You may not fully understand why this is important, but marrying a friend is always easier than trying to turn a spouse into one later. There are significant benefits to marrying your friend—I speak from experience.

BENEFITS OF MARRYING YOUR FRIEND

- **It Eliminates Pretense:**

Marrying your friend allows you to be yourself at all times. You won't feel the need to pretend or put on a façade. For instance, the way you eat, talk, and act around your close friends should not be different when you are with the person you intend to marry. If you still feel shy or uncomfortable around them, it may be a sign that you haven't yet developed a true friendship.

- **It Creates Stronger Intimacy and Connection:**

Before I expand on this, let me ask you a question—do you know that marriage is not just about sex? Some people believe that sex happens every day in marriage, but here's the truth: whether your libido is high or low, sex does not happen every day. Even if, hypothetically, you were intimate daily, it wouldn't last 24 hours. So, what will you do with the remaining hours when you're home with your spouse, especially if you are not friends? Marrying your friend fosters closeness, enhancing both emotional and physical intimacy.

- **It Makes Communication and Expression of Feelings Easier:**

Being married to your friend enables open and honest communication. True friendship means understanding each other's strengths, weaknesses, and values. A genuine friend will not pick at your words or constantly misinterpret your intentions. They will provide a safe and secure space for you to express your feelings without judgement. There will be times when you need to connect, not just as spouses but as friends.

- **It Leads to Better Conflict Resolution:**

Marrying your friend does not mean you won't have arguments or disagreements. However, when conflicts arise, you will find it easier to resolve them without causing lasting damage to the relationship.

- **It Makes Having Fun Together Easier:**

Marrying your friend allows you to embrace your playful, childlike side. After all, everyone has a bit of childlike wonder within them. Marry someone with whom you feel free to joke, laugh, and be silly.

Someone who will laugh at your jokes—even when they aren't particularly funny. This ensures that your home will be filled with joy, rather than dull moments. Fun is essential in marriage; you don't want to be with someone who is always too serious. Every day doesn't need to be rigid. Too much seriousness can make life boring. Choose someone who brings a sense of ease and happiness into your life.

Remember, you can find this companionship within your circle of friends. So, don't automatically "friend zone" everyone. If you think you can't marry someone within your friend group, it may be time to reconsider the kind of friends you surround yourself with.

I understand that marrying your friend may not always be the case for everyone. However, if you're choosing to marry someone who was not originally a friend, it is crucial to intentionally cultivate friendship within your marriage. Friendship is what stands the test of time. I have seen friends get married only to become strangers because they stopped nurturing their friendship after marriage. It is a mistake to assume that your friendship will remain strong without effort. A tree that is not cultivated will not bear good fruit.

WHAT MARRYING YOUR FRIEND IS NOT

- It does not mean you will never have disagreements.
- It does not mean your partner will automatically know everything you want or expect. Communication is still

necessary. Many people experience disappointments because they assume their spouse will just know what they need.

- It does not mean your friendship should end after marriage. Problems arise when people separate friendship from marriage instead of allowing the two to coexist.
- It does not mean you cannot have other friends outside your marriage.
- It should not take away romance from the relationship. If the excitement of romance fades after marriage, something is being done wrong.
- It should not lead to a lack of respect. Some people reject the idea of *marrying their friend* because they believe it will lead to a loss of respect. This is not true. Respect is a choice, and true friendship should foster, not diminish, mutual respect.

While not everyone will marry their friend, I strongly encourage you to build a friendship with the person you are marrying, especially if you have never been friends before. However, remember that not every friend is meant to be a spouse.

So, ask yourself: Is the person I am planning to marry someone I can freely express myself with? Or do I plan to *make* him or her my friend after the wedding? Be honest with yourself, because you don't want to end up with someone you are afraid to talk to or with whom you struggle to have real-life conversations.

In the next chapter, we will discuss communication—why it is crucial in relationships and the dangers of staying silent in a relationship.

4

TALK ABOUT YOUR FUTURE

"Planning is bringing the future into the present so that you can do something about it now."

- Alan Lakein

The courtship stage is the time to discuss the future of your relationship. You cannot afford to avoid important conversations. Communication is key at this stage and in every other stage of marriage, so you need to start practising it now.

WHAT IS COMMUNICATION?

Communication is the act of sharing information from one person to another. Many problems in marriage today stem from a lack of communication. A common example is when the message conveyed by one partner is not received as intended by the other. Another example is remaining silent, assuming that your partner should automatically understand what you want or need. This is dangerous—assumptions have ruined many homes.

To avoid this, talk about the things that matter to you. Don't assume your partner will know. Discuss your present situation and your plans for the future of the relationship. Ask questions; talking is how you truly get to know someone. Avoiding these conversations could lead to surprises later, which can cause problems in marriage.

EXAMPLES OF QUESTIONS TO ASK

Before diving into these questions, I encourage you to answer truthfully. Some people give answers to please their partner, especially out of desperation. I understand you love this person and don't want to lose them, but remember that a marriage built on deception will not last. If you give dishonest answers now and later change your stance, your partner may see you as unreliable. Many marriages fail not because couples didn't ask questions, but because some answers were not given honestly.

Of course, some answers may change due to circumstances beyond your control, but the fundamental values that matter most to you should remain consistent.

There is no need to lie about what you want in your marriage if you truly wish to enjoy it. If your partner's values do not align with yours, it's better to recognize this early and find ways to compromise. Be honest during courtship because the truth will not stay hidden forever. Also, keep in mind that flexibility is not easy for everyone. Identify your non-negotiables. If you assume your partner will be flexible and they are not, what will happen then?

Now that you understand the importance of answering these questions truthfully, here are some important ones to discuss:

1. What does "home" mean to you?

Your perception of a home might differ from your partner's because you were not raised in the same environment. Discussing this question will help you understand your partner's upbringing and expectations. If one or both of you grew up in a toxic home, this conversation can help you determine how to build a better, healthier home together.

2. What could make your love for me fade?

This question should never be overlooked because love is not always constant—certain situations or behaviors can cause feelings to change. If you think this is not possible, ask yourself: *Why do couples who were once in love end up hating each other or even getting divorced after a few years or months of marriage?*

Most people who get married do so out of love, not force. So, what goes wrong? Where does the "butterfly in the belly" feeling go? You've probably seen couples who act like strangers or even enemies. While love should ideally be unconditional, certain actions—intended or not—can affect how your partner feels about you. Knowing what could change their love for you allows both of you to set expectations and prevent avoidable problems in your marriage.

3. How do we handle our finances?

Financial discussions are a must in any relationship. The way you manage your finances can either bring you closer or create division. There is no one-size-fits-all approach. It depends on what you and your partner agree on.

For instance, some women believe their money is theirs alone, while their husband's money belongs to both of them. As a man, do you agree with this? Is this the financial arrangement you envision for your future marriage? Others believe in a strict 50/50 split—what are your thoughts on this? Discussing finances now will help set clear expectations and prevent future conflicts.

4. How do we handle in-laws?

Navigating relationships with in-laws is crucial because you don't want to be the reason your partner's relationship with their family deteriorates. Talk about how to balance relationships with in-laws while setting healthy boundaries. Issues with in-laws can strain a couple's love if not managed properly. Ask how your partner feels about maintaining a strong yet respectful connection with both families while ensuring no one interferes in your marriage.

5. How many children do we want to have?

While this decision may change due to various circumstances, discussing it early will give you an idea of your partner's preferences. If your expectations differ, you can find a middle ground. Marriage requires flexibility—anyone with a rigid mindset may struggle to enjoy it. Additionally, discuss parenting styles and how you both envision raising your children.

6. Where do we want to live?

What are your thoughts on starting small and building over time? Some people are comfortable beginning their family in a one-bedroom apartment, while others insist on a three-bedroom home or nothing less. Understanding each other's expectations about living arrangements will help you align your plans and avoid disappointments.

7. What type of wedding do we want?

This question is important for women, as many have specific dreams and fantasies about their wedding day. Men, on the other hand, often take a more practical approach. Since the wedding day is considered special, it's important to discuss expectations to prevent surprises.

As a man, understanding your partner's vision for the wedding will help you prepare accordingly. As a woman, knowing your partner's thoughts on the wedding will help you set realistic expectations and avoid planning beyond your budget. Marriage is not just about the wedding day; it's about the life you build afterwards.

8. What jobs or businesses do we have?

This is a crucial question because financial stability matters in marriage. I won't sugarcoat it—money is important. Anyone who tells you otherwise is not being truthful.

You don't necessarily need a high-paying corporate job, but you should have a source of income, no matter how small. Financial struggles can lead to frustration in marriage, so both partners should be doing something to contribute to the household.

9. Do we plan to have children in the first year of marriage?

Pregnancy is something you want to be prepared for. While you cannot control exactly when it happens, discussing it beforehand helps set expectations—especially for the woman, who will carry the pregnancy. If a woman is not mentally or emotionally prepared for pregnancy, it can lead to a difficult experience. Have an open conversation about when you both would like to start a family.

10. What are our spiritual beliefs and values?

Spiritual beliefs should not be taken lightly because they play a significant role in navigating the journey of marriage. Marriage cannot be sustained by knowledge and strength alone; you will need spiritual strength to overcome challenges.

If you choose to run your marriage based on biblical principles and follow them rightly, you should expect a strong and fulfilling relationship. Some of these principles can be found in the book of Ephesians in the Bible. Discuss your spiritual perspectives with your partner to ensure alignment in values and beliefs.

11. Ask Questions About Health Status

These critical questions should never be ignored, as they can have a profound impact on your future. Ignorance about essential information, particularly regarding health, is not an option.

For instance, you must know both your genotype and your partner's. Additionally, both of you should get tested for STDs (sexually transmitted diseases), fertility, and genetic disorders before planning a wedding. Understanding your partner's health status is crucial because any negative consequences may not only affect you but also your future children.

This knowledge will help you prepare for what lies ahead if you move forward. When you are informed, there will be no surprises. While faith plays a role in many aspects of life, it is important to ask yourself whether your faith alone is enough to handle potential health challenges.

Your current feelings may not matter as much when real problems arise. Do not allow love to blind you from checking everything that needs to be checked. I have seen cases where both partners had the AS genotype, and their struggles began when they started having children with sickle cell anemia. This not only placed a financial and emotional strain on their relationship but also caused immense suffering for their children due to their parents' lack of foresight.

Furthermore, ensure the information your partner provides is truthful. If you discover a health issue but still choose to proceed with the relationship, both of you will at least be prepared for what to expect. This way, there will be no misunderstandings or conflicts regarding health matters later on.

5

MENTAL BELIEFS

"Your beliefs become your thoughts. Your thoughts become your words. Your words become your actions. Your actions become your habits. Your habits become your values. Your values become your destiny."

- Mahatma Gandhi

In this chapter, we will discuss certain mental beliefs about marriage that often influence how people react to or handle their relationships. Many misconceptions exist about both marriage and the individuals involved, and these false beliefs can be damaging.

These mental beliefs often create a mental block in people's minds. When it comes to marriage, our preconceived notions about how it should function play a crucial role. This is because the way a marriage is run is largely dependent on the beliefs that have already been formed in the hearts of those involved.

At times, these beliefs make it difficult for married individuals to accept advice from counsellors, especially when the guidance contradicts what they have always believed. The issue is that such beliefs create a fixed mindset, making counselling ineffective for some couples. However, when mental beliefs are positive, they can be beneficial for both partners.

A person's mindset can either be positive or negative, depending on what they were exposed to while growing up. If their preconceptions align with the principles written in God's manual, it becomes easier for counselors to provide guidance during challenging times.

These beliefs are shaped by various factors—how we were raised, what we observed while growing up, and the marriages of those around us. Some of these beliefs are positive, while others are negative and can damage a relationship. In this chapter, I will focus on the negative beliefs that can harm a marriage. There are many, but I will discuss thirteen of them in this section.

1. **"All Men Cheat"**

The first negative mental belief I want to address is the notion that *all men cheat.* Many women hold this belief, but it is completely false. Just because some men cheat does not mean all men do. Accepting this mindset is dangerous because it can increase the likelihood of it becoming your reality.

When a man senses that cheating isn't a big deal to you or that you already expect it, it can unconsciously give him a sense of permission to be irresponsible. Your mindset is a powerful tool—it can either elevate or bring you down. If you have been thinking this way, I urge you to change your perspective. Cheating is wrong, regardless of gender, and a person who truly loves and respects their partner will remain faithful.

While some men lack self-control that does not mean *every* man does. There are still faithful, committed men out there. Women must recognize their worth and stop allowing false beliefs to shape their expectations. And let's not forget; women cheat too. If you believe *all* men cheat, ask yourself: are you a cheater as well?

2. "Marriage is a Scam"

The second negative mental belief is the idea that *marriage is a scam*. Marriage itself is not a scam—the only time it becomes one is when either one or both partners enter it with deceitful intentions.

So, ask yourself: *Are you a scammer? Are you entering marriage to deceive your partner?* If your answer is no, then your marriage will not be a scam, just as mine and many others are not. Marriage is what the people involved make of it. If both you and your partner are honest and committed, why would you contribute to the false notion that marriage is a scam?

People who believe this often do so because they are unprepared for the realities of marriage or because one or both partners failed to prioritize each other's well-being. A marriage in which one or both partners are selfish will always feel like a scam. If you are certain about the person you are planning to marry, have faith that your marriage will not be a scam. Do not judge your future based on the negative experiences of others. Using someone else's bad experience as a blueprint for your marriage is a dangerous mistake.

3. "Women Are Evil and More Dangerous Than a Snake"

The third harmful belief is the idea that *women are evil and more dangerous than snakes*. This is a complete lie, and it is wrong to believe such a statement. As a man, ask yourself: *Have all the women in my life been evil?* If the answer is no, then why would you believe those who claim that *all* women are evil? Surely, if you have encountered good women, you know this belief cannot be true.

Not all women are evil. The problem may be the type of person someone chooses to be involved with. As a single man, do not let this false belief scare you. Instead, focus on choosing the right partner. The key is to avoid relationships with individuals who do not align with your values and intentions.

4. "Once You Are Married, the Spark Dies"

The fourth negative belief I want to address is the idea that *once you are married, the spark dies.* This belief is one of the reasons many people fear marriage. It is also why some individuals prefer to live together without making a formal commitment.

Marriage should never stop partners from being intentional about keeping the spark alive or expressing love toward one another. Love does not sustain itself automatically; it requires effort. Couples must learn to nurture their love continuously so it can grow and flourish over time.

5. "Women Need to Be Beaten to Reset Their Brains"

The fifth harmful belief is the idea that *women need to be beaten to reset their brains.* This is a wrong and dangerous mindset for any man to have. Just because you grew up witnessing men in your environment beating their wives does not make it right. Abuse is never a sign of strength; it is a sign of weakness. Strong men do not resort to violence to assert control.

If you ever saw your mother being abused, how did you feel? Were you happy about it, or did it make you bitter toward your father? If it hurt you then, why would you want the same thing to happen in your home?

There is no excuse for a man to lay hands on his wife, no matter the situation. Marriage should be a place of love, respect, and partnership and not a place for physical violence or dominance.

6. "Marriage Is a Place of Death"

The sixth negative belief stems from the wedding vow that states, *"Till death do us part".* Some people misunderstand this phrase, thinking it means they must endure suffering in silence, even in toxic or dangerous marriages. Others believe that marriage is only about joy and pleasure, and the moment challenges arise, they feel justified in leaving.

Let me make this clear: *marriage is not a place of death.* It is meant to be a lifelong commitment built on love, respect, and mutual support. However, this does not mean you should stay in a marriage where your life is in danger.

As much as I value and advocate for marriage, I do not support the idea that one must stay in a relationship that is physically, emotionally, or mentally abusive. No one should ever lose their life because of marriage.

Marriage is not a ticket to heaven, and if your safety is at risk, you must seek help. Do not stay in a harmful situation out of fear of what others might say. Too many people have lost their lives due to toxic and abusive marriages—you do not want to be another example.

Remember, *the covenant of life is more important than the covenant of marriage.* While marriage is a beautiful institution, it should never come at the cost of your well-being or safety. If you find yourself in an abusive situation, prioritize your life and seek help.

7. "Marriage is Hard or Difficult"

It is understandable that some people fear marriage due to the negative things they have heard from those who are already married. In fact, some married individuals advise singles not to get married, claiming that it is too difficult. The irony, however, is that many of these people remain married themselves.

Would you like to know the truth? The truth is that marriage requires effort, but it is not impossible. If you are not willing to invest the time, energy, and intention it demands, you will undoubtedly struggle, just as you would in any other area of life where you fail to take the necessary steps to succeed. People often complain when they are not getting the outcomes they expected, even when they are not approaching things correctly.

The same principle applies to marriage. Let us stop assigning a negative label to something God never intended to be viewed negatively. Marriage is not something that operates on autopilot after the wedding day. You and your partner must be committed to working together to build the kind of future you both desire.

God has provided the roadmap—His principles. But you and your spouse are the drivers. So, consider this: Is the person you are planning to journey with as capable and intentional a driver as you are?

Always remember, real marriage begins after the wedding day.

8. "It Is Better to Be Single Than Married"

Whenever I hear someone make this statement, I often smile. Most of the time, such declarations are rooted in negative personal experiences, either from poor past decisions or from the disappointments of others within their circle. In essence, these opinions are typically based on pain, whether directly or indirectly.

You will never hear someone who is happily married say that it is better to remain single. Why? Because they are enjoying the fruits, blessings, and fulfillment that a healthy marriage brings. This is the perspective you should seek—not one shaped by bitterness or regret, but by hope, joy, and purpose.

Many who believe that being single is better often change their minds when they encounter someone who treats them with genuine love and respect. Suddenly, their previously firm stance begins to soften. Even individuals who once strongly identified as independent or anti-marriage tend to reevaluate their views when real love enters their lives.

Marriage is, and will always be, a blessing when both partners are committed to making it so. Therefore, do not let the experiences or opinions of others dissuade you from something God designed to be beautiful.

9. "Marriage Is a Prison or Bondage"

This is a misconception. Marriage is not about losing your freedom, and it is certainly not a form of bondage. While there are some changes and responsibilities that come with marriage, they signify growth, not restriction.

In marriage, you are no longer living solely for yourself. You become responsible for another person and are expected to be accountable to your spouse. This is why marriage is not for those who are irresponsible or self-centered. If you are not yet ready to care for someone else, bringing them into your life could lead to unnecessary frustration for both of you.

One reason some individuals resist the idea of marriage is that they do not want to be accountable to anyone, yet they still desire the benefits of marriage. The truth is, you cannot separate accountability from a healthy marital union.

Marriage unites two individuals into one in the sight of God. For example, informing your spouse of your whereabouts is not about control—it is about love, safety, and wisdom. In case of an emergency, your spouse should be able to locate or support you.

So, ask yourself: Are you truly ready and willing to be accountable to the person you are considering marrying? Because accountability is one of the foundational aspects of doing marriage the right way.

Marriage is not a prison—it is a purposeful partnership.

10. "There Is No Value in a Wedding Certificate"

Although a wedding certificate is printed on paper, it should never be viewed as just another document. It is a legally binding proof that you are officially married to your spouse. This is why it is often required for critical life decisions such as immigration applications, joint property purchases, or accessing spousal benefits.

The wedding certificate holds significant value and is taken seriously by legal institutions around the world. In any system that functions properly, it carries more authority than many people realize.

It is true that in some countries, the importance of this document has been devalued, and as a result, many no longer pursue it. However, in developed nations and structured societies, it still holds considerable legal, financial, and social relevance.

11. "Women Are Difficult to Please"

Who says this—and why do people believe it? The statement is simply untrue. Yes, some individuals are difficult to please, but this is not exclusive to women.

The reason some believe this myth is because they have not encountered men who are also hard to satisfy. The truth is, there are people, regardless of gender, who are never content, no matter what is done for them.

What truly matters is your ability to discern the nature of the person you are involved with. During courtship, take the time to observe whether your partner is appreciative or constantly dissatisfied. These are signs you should not ignore, as they often carry into marriage.

This issue is not about gender—it is about individual personality and emotional maturity.

12. "You Shouldn't Tell Your Spouse About Your Past"

This is another myth that is rooted in fear and misunderstanding. The only time your past becomes a problem is when you are dealing with an emotionally immature partner. It takes a lack of maturity for someone to weaponize your history during moments of conflict.

Unfortunately, some people do this, which is why it is essential to get to know the person you intend to marry before disclosing deeply personal information. Trust must be earned—it cannot be rushed. You should not open up to someone you've just met. Emotional safety is built over time.

In my own marriage, my husband and I know everything about each other, both the positive and the painful. Yet, we have never used those truths against one another.

So, the question is: Has this person earned the level of trust required for you to share your past? Are they emotionally equipped to receive it with grace and understanding? Without trust, openness becomes risky. And in any lasting relationship, trust and maturity are non-negotiable foundations.

13. "As a Lady, You Can't Fulfill Your Purpose After Marriage"

This is a dangerous lie from the pit of hell. Marriage should never hinder a woman from fulfilling the call of God upon her life. Every individual—man or woman—has a divine purpose. Marriage is part of your earthly assignment, but it is not the totality of your identity or calling.

Your marriage should function as a ministry—one that reflects God's intention and inspires others. While not everyone experiences this reality, that doesn't mean it's not possible. Each marriage is unique.

In fact, marriage should empower you to do more than you ever could on your own. The Bible declares, "One shall chase a thousand, and two shall put ten thousand to flight." When unity and agreement exist between husband and wife, there should be exponential growth.

According to God's design, you are not supposed to remain stagnant after marriage. There should be evident spiritual, emotional, and personal development, especially where love, unity, selflessness, and generosity are present.

Marriage is not your only purpose, even though it is a significant part of your life journey. Be mindful of the messages you internalize, the voices you listen to, and the lives you admire.

Never accept the lie that you cannot fulfill your purpose after marriage. If you believe that lie, it may become your reality—but it doesn't have to. Reject it, and walk confidently in the truth: God's purpose for your life remains valid and powerful, regardless of your marital status.

6

INTENTIONALITY AND DETERMINATION

"Therefore a man shall leave his father and his mother and hold fast to his wife, and they shall become one flesh."

- Genesis 2:24

Asking all the right questions, and attending premarital counselling are not the only things required to build a good home. Another important question to consider is: **Are you prepared and determined for the journey ahead?**

Marriage requires effort, and you must be willing to put in the work to see beautiful results. This is why I named my ministry *The Doing Couple*—because a successful marriage does not happen on its own; it requires active participation from both partners.

The marriages you admire and desire did not just happen by chance. If you ask those couples what they do differently, you will discover that their **intentionality** is what has produced the results you admire today. The commitment between both partners is what has brought them to where they are now. No marriage achieves success without a firm **determination** to make it work. It is this determination that keeps couples from giving up during life's challenges.

To truly enjoy your marriage, you must have the mindset that you are in it to make it work. This level of determination prevents you from seeing **divorce** as an easy way out when issues arise. Intentionality and determination must come from both partners because marriage will not always be smooth. If only one partner is committed to making the marriage work, their efforts will be frustrating and unsustainable during difficult times.

Marriage is a place of **service**, and both partners must be willing to serve each other for the relationship to thrive. Therefore, marriage is not an institution to enter without **determination, intentionality, and preparation**. You need to be **mentally, psychologically, and physically prepared**.

MENTAL AND PSYCHOLOGICAL PREPARATION

You must be mentally prepared and determined to make your marriage work. There will be **unexpected challenges** that may cause disagreements, but these are often growth opportunities. Some situations that cause misunderstandings early in marriage will eventually become things you laugh about in the future. They happen because they help you understand each other better.

The reason some people easily walk away from marriage at the first sign of trouble is that they were never prepared for the realities of marriage. But your case will be different—because you are taking the time to prepare by reading this book.

Misunderstandings will happen, and that is normal. It doesn't matter how deeply you love your spouse; disagreements are inevitable.

For example, in my marriage, my husband and I once argued about how to cook beans. He had a particular method he preferred, but when he tried to show me, I refused to listen because I felt his way took too much time and effort, while mine was quicker and more straightforward. The issue was resolved when he cooked the beans himself a few times using his method. I must admit, his method was better and tasted more scrumptious! After practicing his way, I became the best at it—I even cook it better than he does now. Today, it's an inside joke between us whenever I make beans.

Now, ask yourself: *Should a disagreement over cooking beans have led to a misunderstanding?* Of course not! But it did despite the love we have for each other.

I have also heard of couples arguing over **how to squeeze toothpaste**! These little things can cause disagreements, so be prepared for yours. When you are mentally prepared, you will understand that **misunderstandings should not break you**.

The mindset I want you to develop ahead of time is that you are not in marriage to back out at the first sign of trouble. When disagreements happen, your first option should never be divorce.

There is something called **forbearance**—the ability to endure and tolerate others' shortcomings. This is an essential skill for every aspect of life, but especially in marriage. If you do not master the skill of tolerance, you will face **constant conflict** in your marriage.

In marriage, you must be willing to accept each other's flaws because no one is perfect. Everyone has strengths and weaknesses. If you only focus on your partner's weaknesses, you will fail to appreciate their strengths and what they bring to the relationship. So, ask yourself: *Am I ready to accept this person's flaws? Have I identified their weaknesses so I can learn how to complement them?*

SKILLS TO DEVELOP FOR MENTAL AND PSYCHOLOGICAL PREPARATION

To better prepare yourself, here are essential skills you should develop:

- Communication skills (especially listening)
- Conflict resolution
- Emotional intelligence
- Forgiveness
- Financial management
- Flexibility
- Commitment
- Intentionality to make it work
- Spirituality
- Self-awareness

7

EXPECTATIONS IN MARRIAGE

He answered, "Have you not read that he who created them from the beginning made them male and female, and said, 'Therefore a man shall leave his father and his mother and hold fast to his wife, and the two shall become one flesh'? So they are no longer two but one flesh. What therefore God has joined together, let not man separate."

- Matthew 19:4-6

Before going further in this chapter, I would like you to reflect on your expectations for the marriage you are planning. Ask yourself questions like, **What are my expectations in this marriage? Are they realistic?**

I emphasize this because many marital issues stem from **unrealistic expectations** placed on one partner by the other. Do you expect to leave the marriage when things don't go as you imagined, or are you committed to staying and fighting for your marriage through life's challenges? There are different types of expectations—both spoken and unspoken.

EXPECTATIONS ABOUT DISAGREEMENTS

Some people believe that once they marry the love of their life, there won't be any challenges. Do you want to hear the truth? **That is a big lie.**

Disagreements are inevitable, and they help you understand your spouse better. It is perfectly normal. You must accept that the person you are madly in love with will not always make you happy.

Early in marriage, you may feel sad or frustrated when your spouse does things differently from what you expected. This is natural because you were both raised in different environments and have developed different habits.

EXPECTATIONS ABOUT FINANCES

What are your expectations regarding the financial status of your future spouse? I ask this because finance is one of the biggest causes of divorce among couples who were once deeply in love.

As a woman, are you truly comfortable with your partner's financial state? Will you later put pressure on him when you start comparing your life to what other men provide for their wives? Will you begin to call him lazy or good for nothing if he doesn't meet your financial expectations?

Think carefully about this. **No man wants to experience that kind of pressure.**

Are you willing to walk through life with your spouse and build something great together? This is often the best kind of relationship, but **are you truly prepared for that journey?** Be honest with yourself—do not let emotions cloud your judgement.

Do not say **"yes"** if you know deep down that you are easily influenced by the lavish lifestyles displayed on social media. Every responsible man who has a bright future and is working towards it values his peace of mind.

EXPECTATIONS ABOUT PHYSICAL APPEARANCE

This section is primarily for men because men are more likely to be influenced by physical appearance.

Ask yourself: **Am I truly okay with how my future wife looks?**

Are you aware that her body will change after childbirth? It would be unfair to ignore this reality, go ahead with wedding plans, and later find yourself drawn to other women you believe have a "perfect shape".

You must understand that pregnancy and childbirth can bring significant changes to a woman's body. She may gain weight, and her breasts may sag. While some women naturally return to their pre-pregnancy shape due to genetics, most experience lasting changes.

So, will you still love and appreciate her when these changes happen?

EXPECTATIONS ABOUT SPIRITUALITY

First, assess your level of spirituality.

- Are you a spiritual person?
- Have you assessed the spiritual level of the person you want to marry?

Some people enter marriage fully aware that their partner is not spiritually inclined, yet they expect them to become more devoted after marriage. This is unrealistic and often leads to conflict.

For example, if your partner did not pray daily before marriage, why would you expect them to suddenly start praying every day after marriage? If they struggled to pray for 10 minutes before, expecting them to pray for 30 minutes to an hour after marriage is unreasonable.

This does not mean people cannot grow, but spiritual growth takes time and requires patience. Marriage will not magically change someone's habits.

Another important question to ask yourself is: **Does my partner have a growth mindset?**

A person with a growth mindset will be open to personal and spiritual development, while someone with a **fixed mindset** may resist change and frustrate your efforts.

THE IMPORTANCE OF CONVICTION

The final and most important thing is to be fully convinced that this person is right for you. When you are truly convinced, you will experience inner peace.

However, if your conviction is based purely on emotions rather than deep certainty, be prepared to face the consequences.

MY PERSONAL EXPERIENCE

One of the biggest risks my husband took was **marrying me**.

I was raised in a **Muslim household** and was very devoted to my faith—I prayed five times a day without fail. My father was a Christian, and my mother was a Muslim, but I did not have a Muslim name. I was raised primarily by my mother's family.

Interestingly, my husband's background was similar. He was raised by both Christian and Muslim families, but he identified as **a Christian**.

When we met, I was still a **practicing Muslim**. We became friends, and over time, our friendship deepened into something more. We realized that our **values aligned**, except for one major aspect—**spirituality**.

One day, my husband expressed his feelings for me and told me that he was convinced I was the one for him. However, he also said something important:

"I cannot marry a Muslim. That is the only obstacle".

I took time to **pray** and found an **unexplainable peace**—something I had never felt in my previous relationships. I even asked a close Muslim friend to pray with me.

After praying, my friend gave me advice that brought me even more peace, though he remained concerned about my possible **conversion**. At that point, I surrendered my decision to **God** and asked for guidance.

Eventually, I told my husband that I was **ready to convert** and began attending a nearby church. That was where I **encountered my salvation**—an experience I am forever grateful for.

Today, my faith has grown so much that nothing could ever change it. In fact, at one point in our marriage, I became even more prayerful than my husband.

We are grateful for how everything turned out, but I cannot ignore the **risk** we both took. What if things had turned out differently? What if my conversion had not been genuine? What if I had resented him for influencing my faith?

If things had gone wrong, we both would have faced serious consequences. This is why you must be certain of your decision before getting married.

EXPECTATIONS ABOUT ROMANCE

What are your expectations regarding romance in marriage, and how do they compare to what your partner currently does? Based on your assessment, does your partner meet your standard and definition of romance? Many marriages experience challenges because expectations of romance do not align with reality.

It would be unfair to assume that someone you consider unromantic will suddenly become romantic and affectionate after marriage. This is why it's essential to be clear about your desires and not compromise on your non-negotiables.

I have heard cases where wives complain that their husbands are not romantic because they don't buy gifts like flowers, open car doors, plan dates, cuddle, or prioritize them. While these actions help maintain romance in a marriage, the key question is: does your partner exhibit these behaviors now? If not, do you believe they are open to change?

If they are not naturally inclined towards romantic gestures and are unwilling to adjust, expecting them to change after marriage may lead to frustration. Some people have strong personalities that resist change, which could negatively impact your relationship.

You also need to ensure that your definition of romance is yours and not influenced by others. Be realistic with your expectations.

EXPECTATIONS ABOUT BEING THE CENTRE OF THE MARRIAGE

Do you believe that marriage should revolve solely around you? If so, you may need to reassess your mindset. Marriage involves two people, and it should be a partnership where both individuals feel valued and important.

As a man, do you expect your wife to treat you like a king? While this is ideal, remember that kings marry queens. If you want to be treated like a king, are you prepared to treat your wife as your queen? A woman automatically becomes a queen when she marries a king, but she must also be respected and cherished.

Likewise, many women expect to be treated as queens, but some take it a step further by believing that marriage should revolve entirely around them. This is unfair, as marriage should not favor one person over the other. Both partners should treat each other with mutual love, respect, and consideration.

Ask yourself: Is my partner worthy of being my king or queen?

BEHAVIOURAL EXPECTATIONS

Do you know that good character and Behaviour are more important in marriage than physical appearance?

One of the reasons you must assess this before setting a wedding date is that character greatly influences the success of a marriage. Marrying someone with a bad character can lead to regret and frustration. Similarly, if you have a poor character, your spouse will not enjoy the marriage, and you do not want to be the reason someone thinks marriage is a scam.

Marriage is not a scam—only people who deceive themselves or others create unhappy unions. So, ask yourself: Am I or my future spouse being truthful about our character?

For example, one of my most important criteria for a partner was care and kindness. My husband met this standard—he is caring not just to me but to everyone around him.

EXPECTATIONS ABOUT CHILDREN'S OUTLOOK

Children are a significant aspect of many marriages, and some couples face disappointment when their children's appearance does not match their expectations.

For instance, some women desire light-skinned children even when married to a dark-skinned partner. But what were they expecting when they said, "I do"? Genetics play a crucial role, and children inherit traits from both parents.

Beyond physical traits, children can also inherit behavioral tendencies from either parent. Ask yourself: If my children inherit my partner's personality, will I be happy? If not, is it a trait you can help them manage or correct? Remember, this is one expectation you cannot control.

Another common expectation is regarding gender. Some men blame their wives for giving birth to only daughters, not understanding that gender is determined by the father's chromosome. If you are a man, educate yourself on this biological fact before unfairly blaming your wife. Be prepared to defend her from societal pressure if necessary.

UNDERSTANDING THAT YOU CAN'T CHANGE PEOPLE

Before planning a wedding or saying "I do", understand this fundamental truth: **You cannot change anyone.**

If someone has changed because of your influence, it is not because of your power but because they chose to change. People change when they want to—not because someone else forces them to.

Women, in particular, often make the mistake of thinking they can change men. Many women marry partners they know are not right for them, believing they will change after marriage. This illusion has led to many unhappy marriages.

No one is indeed perfect, but you must identify your non-negotiables before committing. Ask yourself: If this person never changes, will their Behaviour affect my love for them? If the answer is yes, reconsider your decision.

*I have seen many cases where women expected their partners to change after marriage, only to be disappointed. Some now regret their choices, and I am sure you do not want to find yourself in a similar situation.

For example, if anger management is crucial to you, avoid marrying someone prone to destructive outbursts. If they do not change, their aggression may one day be directed at you. Similarly, if you dislike drinking or smoking, marrying someone with these habits may lead to conflict in the future.

Some people try to force change on their partners through threats or ultimatums. While this may result in temporary compliance, is that the kind of change you want in the long run? Genuine change must come from within.

Do not assume that a womanizer, a lazy person, or someone with bad hygiene will suddenly transform after marriage. Marriage does not change people—only personal decisions do.

FINAL THOUGHTS

The purpose of this chapter is to help you **fully understand what you are getting into** before marriage. Many people later label their spouse a bad person when, in reality, their expectations were simply unrealistic from the start.

Be honest with yourself about what you can and cannot accept in a marriage. If you are expecting a significant change from your partner, consider whether you can truly handle it if they never change.

Marriage should be built on mutual understanding, respect, and realistic expectations. Choose wisely, and ensure that your expectations align with reality before making a lifelong commitment.

8

PLANS BEFORE PICKING A WEDDING DATE

"An excellent wife who can find? She is far more precious than jewels."

- **Proverbs 31:10**

Now that we have discussed the important things to consider before choosing a wedding date, this chapter and the following ones will focus on the necessary steps to take after confirming that the person you are with is the right one for you.

Before you finalize a wedding date, I want to ask you one last time: Do you have peace within yourself about moving forward with this person? Are you truly ready to commit to a lifetime together? Can you walk the journey of forever with them? If your answer to all these questions is yes, then you are good to go. With that, I would like to be among the first to congratulate you!

Congratulations on this incredible journey you are about to embark on!

However, before fixing a wedding date, there are still some essential steps that should not be overlooked. No matter how perfect your partner may seem, unresolved issues can create loopholes that may lead to challenges later on.

PREMARITAL COUNSELLING

The first step for both of you should be scheduling a premarital counselling session with a professional. This is where you will learn practical ways to navigate marriage successfully. When I say premarital counselling, I am not referring to a rushed session that lasts only two weeks, as some people do.

I find it amusing when engaged couples say they don't have enough time for counselling but can make time for dance rehearsals, elaborate proposals, and bachelor or bachelorette parties. Some even claim they can't afford counselling sessions yet spend large sums on extravagant wedding events. I am not saying you shouldn't celebrate your wedding in a memorable way if you have the resources. But don't you think it's unwise to invest heavily in a one-day event while neglecting something that will help build a strong and lasting marriage? Better knowledge leads to a better experience.

If you want to be intentional about having a good marriage, it should start now. I'm sure you don't want to wait until problems arise before seeking professional guidance.

Many churches offer counselling sessions for engaged couples, which is a good idea—provided the counsellors are properly trained. Being a pastor does not automatically qualify someone to provide effective marriage counselling. Thankfully, many churches today are investing in training their pastors to ensure they can properly counsel engaged couples.

Regardless of where you seek guidance, the most important thing is to learn from someone who teaches biblical principles and does not promote unhealthy or misleading views about marriage. You cannot ignore God's design for marriage and expect it to go well because He is the creator of marriage. Unfortunately, many couples overlook this step, which is why some struggle in the early stages of marriage.

ADVANTAGES OF PREMARITAL COUNSELLING

1. It provides practical strategies for building a successful marriage.
2. It helps couples understand common challenges faced in the early stages of marriage.
3. It prepares couples for potential issues that often lead to conflict.
4. It clarifies the roles of a husband and wife in marriage.
5. It offers guidance on strengthening emotional and physical intimacy.
6. It teaches conflict resolution skills—because disagreements are inevitable.
7. It helps couples understand what it truly means to be united as one.
8. It gives insight into your partner's thoughts and expectations, especially during counselling discussions.
9. It allows counselors to help manage unrealistic expectations before they become a problem.
10. It educates couples—both virgins and non-virgins—on navigating their first sexual experiences in marriage.

And these are just a few of the many benefits.

Whether you choose to complete counseling before or after setting a wedding date is up to you as a couple. However, what's most important is that the counselling happens before the wedding day. There have been cases where couples separated after counseling because they realized they had fundamental disagreements that should have been addressed long before reaching this stage.

WHAT TO DO AFTER SETTING A WEDDING DATE

- **Learn to Work Together as a Team**

Some couples allow their family or friends to influence their wedding planning decisions, which often leads to unnecessary conflict. One partner may become upset if changes are made to plans they had previously agreed on. To prevent this, engaged couples should ensure that no one influences them against each other.

The key is for both partners to first agree on what they want for their wedding. It is their special day, and they should have the final say. This becomes even easier when the couple is primarily responsible for financing their wedding.

This does not mean you should ignore the opinions of family and friends entirely. If their suggestions align with what you and your partner want, that's great. However, if their advice contradicts your mutual decisions, you must be firm in saying no politely but confidently. Defending your decisions together is an important first step in building a strong and united marriage.

You do not need to please anyone at the expense of your partner's happiness. If you stand firm in your decisions, some people may not like it, but this will help establish healthy boundaries. It will also send a clear message: you and your partner are a united team that cannot be easily divided.

- **Pray for Each Other**

Another crucial step is to commit the journey ahead into God's hands. Pray for each other and together, asking God to provide the resources you need. Also, pray for the wisdom necessary for a smooth and successful marriage. You will need wisdom to navigate life together with ease.

Pray for good weather on your wedding day and the safe travels of all guests, so that they may return to their destinations without accident. I'm sure you want your wedding day to be remembered for good reasons. Imagine if some of your guests were involved in an accident—it would forever be a painful memory for their families.

Also, pray against any evil plans that may be directed toward your special day. If you and your partner can fast and pray for your wedding day, I strongly encourage you to do so—fasting will not harm you. Additionally, you can pray about other aspects that may not have been mentioned here.

Your wedding day is not merely an entertainment event, even though there will be activities to celebrate the occasion. Do not focus solely on entertainment while neglecting the necessity of prayer. Marriage is not just a physical union; it is also spiritual and should be taken seriously. Some forces do not want you to have peace or succeed in marriage, so you must be determined and ready to entrust both your wedding and your marriage into God's hands. Remember, the enemy does not want to see you succeed because he does not want good seeds to come from your union.

Another reason prayer is essential is that people carry different spiritual burdens, and if not rebuked, these can later affect your home. Some of these include the spirit of anger, infidelity, greed, pride, dishonesty, stubbornness, anti-marriage influences, poverty, and many more.

The importance of prayer before and after choosing a wedding date cannot be overemphasized.

This is why 1 Thessalonians 5:17-18 states: *"Be unceasing and persistent in prayer; in every situation be thankful and continually give thanks to God".* And Luke 18:1 says: *"Jesus told a parable to His disciples to show them that they should always pray and not give up".*

This shows that prayer is not only for difficult times—it should be a consistent part of your life. Build your appetite for prayer, and make it a foundation for your marriage.

Confessions for Your Wedding Day

- ✓ Our day is blessed.
- ✓ Everything that happens on this day (mention the date) will work in our favor.
- ✓ Men and women will favor us.
- ✓ There shall be no evil occurrence on that day.
- ✓ Anyone with an evil agenda will not attend our wedding.
- ✓ Our wedding day will be filled with joy and remembered for good.
- ✓ Our home is fruitful.
- ✓ No evil will have dominion over our home.
- ✓ My partner and I dwell in God's wisdom.

- **Talk About Budget**

A wedding day is a special occasion in the life of an engaged couple—a day many singles dream about. Some even spend time fantasizing about every detail. Of course, it's natural to desire a glamorous and memorable celebration.

However, let me ask you an important question: That dream wedding—can you and your partner afford it? Are you planning to go into debt just to make it a reality?

I ask because I have heard too many stories of people borrowing money to fund their weddings. Remember, marriage is meant to be *"till death do us part,"* not *"till debt do us part"*. Going into debt for a wedding is not a wise decision.

Why plan a wedding beyond your means? Who are you trying to impress? Are you doing it for people who, after the wedding, won't contribute anything to your life?

Here's what you need to know: Marriage comes with responsibilities—both planned and unexpected. You must be wise enough to plan for the future within your financial capacity. Most of the people who attend your wedding won't remember every little detail and even if they do, it won't change anything for them.

Sometimes, family members may pressure you into having an extravagant wedding beyond your budget. If that happens, be firm about your limits. Let them know your financial boundaries, and if they want something more elaborate, they should cover the extra costs themselves. After the wedding, when financial struggles arise, those same family members may not offer much support. By then, you and your spouse will no longer be seen as the *"small boy"* or *"small girl"* they once knew—you will be responsible for your home.

So, please be prudent with your wedding budget and plan wisely with your partner. *Cut your coat according to your clothes.* You can have a beautiful and meaningful wedding without overspending. If this means reducing the guest list, so be it. It's better to apologize later to those who weren't invited than to spend years repaying debts from a one-day event.

If you have excess funds, consider saving them for your future together rather than spending everything in one day. You don't want to find yourself struggling financially immediately after the wedding.

- **A Joint Financial Responsibility**

It is not solely the man's responsibility to finance the wedding—both partners should contribute to making their special day beautiful. The financial burden should not rest entirely on the groom.

For brides, if you notice that your family's dowry demands are excessive; you can step in and speak with them. Let them know it is too much and ask them to reduce it. This will help ease the financial strain on your partner.

- **Talk About Those Who Will Be in Charge of Important Tasks**

You need to learn to delegate wedding-related tasks to people you trust—those you are confident can handle them well. Just because someone is a family member does not mean they are the right person for the job. Trust is key when choosing who will be responsible for important aspects of your wedding.

If you can afford a wedding planner, I highly recommend hiring one, as it will save you from unnecessary stress. Wedding planners don't have to be expensive; look for one that fits your budget.

Simply assigning critical responsibilities such as coordinating special guests, taking pictures, or handling video coverage to family members without ensuring they are capable can lead to frustration or disappointment. If they don't follow your instructions properly, it could negatively impact your mood. You don't want anything to dampen your joy or allow anyone to make you feel stressed or upset. Your wedding day is a once-in-a-lifetime event—once it's gone, you cannot relive it.

Also, keep in mind that no matter how perfectly you plan, people can still disappoint you. Human beings are not perfect, and mistakes are bound to happen. However, do not let anyone's errors or shortcomings ruin your mood. Stay focused on the joy of the day.

- **Agreement on Your Wedding Day Look**

This is a topic that is often overlooked, especially by brides. Many women assume that it is their day and that they can dress however they like. However, something as seemingly small as this can be the beginning of issues in some marriages.

For example, if your fiancé is not comfortable with heavy makeup or revealing outfits, it could make him feel uneasy or even irritated on the wedding day. If your husband-to-be has specific preferences regarding your appearance, it's important to discuss and agree on this in advance. Your goal should be to look attractive *to* your spouse, not just to your guests.

On the other hand, if your fiancé does not have any particular concerns about your wedding look, then you have more freedom to choose your style. However, this should not be an excuse to dress inappropriately. Modesty is a virtue often associated with elegance and royalty.

- **Involving Both Families in Wedding Activities**

Another issue that sometimes arises between families is the selection of people for key wedding roles such as the flower girl, ring bearer, and bridal train. While this may not always be a problem, it *can* create unnecessary tension if not handled carefully.

You don't want your partner's family to feel excluded or believe that you are favoring your relatives over theirs. The best and wisest approach is to ensure representation from both families. This way, no one feels left out, and there is less chance of conflict.

If certain family members are unable to afford the required attire or accessories for their roles, they are less likely to feel resentment if they were at least considered for participation. Open communication and thoughtful decision-making can help prevent unnecessary drama on your special day.

9

THE WEDDING DAY

"A successful marriage requires falling in love many times, always with the same person."

- Mignon McLaughlin

On this special and beautiful day, there are some important assignments I would like to give you both:

LET YOUR GAZE BE ON YOUR PARTNER

On your wedding day, your focus and attention should be on your partner, not on anything else. Paying close attention to your spouse will help you notice if they start feeling uneasy due to tasks not being handled properly by those they entrusted with responsibilities. When this happens, you will be able to calm them down before it negatively affects them.

Your wedding photos will become lasting memories, so do not let anyone or anything ruin those moments for you. The reason I am emphasizing this is to prepare your mind ahead of time.

LOOK OUT FOR ONE ANOTHER

Make sure to check on your spouse, especially when it comes to eating. They may not feel like eating, but encourage them to do so. During celebrations, people often forget to eat because they are too focused on ensuring that guests are satisfied. While it's great to be hospitable, you and your partner must also take care of yourselves.

No matter how little, make sure to eat and drink something. If your spouse is uncomfortable eating in front of guests, you can plan to do so privately in the car. This should be discussed and planned before the wedding day.

SMILE

Your genuine smile is important because you never know when the photographer will capture a moment. Your wedding pictures will serve as cherished memories, and you want them to reflect happiness and joy. Focus on things that bring a smile to your face rather than anything that might steal your joy.

KISSING

When the time comes to kiss your spouse, do it passionately—do not make it look forced. Be proud of the person you are marrying. I have seen couples kiss at their wedding as if their partner irritates them, which is not a good look.

Most times, the excuse is that they feel shy kissing in front of their parents and guests. However, since you are preparing yourself ahead of time, I am sure you will handle it differently. In fact, your parents expect you to do it because kissing is part of the ceremony. So, do it confidently, in a way that even the guests will see the love between you both.

This is something you will likely discuss during premarital counselling, as it is an important part of the wedding.

Another common excuse is that some people feel nauseated by kissing. If that is the case, keep mint candy in your pocket (for men) or your purse (for women) to freshen your breath before the moment arrives.

REMAIN CALM

I understand that things may not go as planned, but please, do not let that cause unnecessary agitation. If certain guests who hold a special place in your heart are not treated the way you intended, do not worry. They will be fine. Missing out on food or special treatment for one day will not harm them.

If you feel it is necessary, you can call them later to apologize. Alternatively, you and your spouse can take them out on another day or invite them over after your honeymoon. A reasonable person will understand that you cannot personally cater to every guest during the wedding.

AVOID LATENESS

Lateness is often inevitable at African weddings due to numerous activities and family traditions. However, with proper planning and structure, this can be managed better. Being late creates unnecessary pressure for both the bride and groom, which can affect your mood and emotions. Do your best to avoid delays so you can fully enjoy your special day without stress.

NEVER ALLOW FAMILY MISUNDERSTANDINGS TO AFFECT YOU

Not every family experiences conflicts during weddings, but it can happen. If it does, do not let it affect you. There may be disagreements over seating arrangements or which family members receive certain privileges—just as I shared in Chapter 1 of this book.

If such issues arise, the best thing you and your spouse can do is ignore them. Let family members settle their differences on their own. When they see the strong bond between you two, they will realize that their conflicts cannot break your union.

10

DON'T STOP LEARNING

"Love is patient and kind; love does not envy or boast; it is not arrogant or rude. It does not insist on its own way; it is not irritable or resentful; it does not rejoice at wrongdoing, but rejoices with the truth. Love bears all things, believes all things, hopes all things, endures all things."

- 1 Corinthians 13:4-7

Congratulations once again on this new journey you have embarked on! I pray that your home will be filled with love, joy, and peace. May your marriage be a heaven-on-earth experience. May your home bring glory to God, just as He intended from the beginning. May you never be among those who say marriage is a scam because yours will not be. Your marriage will be so fulfilling and effortless that you and your spouse will become role models for those yet to marry. Amen!

I want you to know that these prayers are not just mere words; by the special grace of God, they will be your reality in marriage. Amen! However, for this to happen, there are certain things you must be intentional about:

First, after your wedding, ensure that God remains the center of your marriage. Any marriage that lacks the presence of God will struggle.

Second, never stop learning how to improve your marriage. Keep doing what you are doing now—reading books. You can also learn by listening to counselors who teach about marriage and relationships based on principles from the ultimate guide, the Bible, and from God Himself.

However, be cautious about whom you listen to on social media. There are many counselors today, and if you are not careful, some may do more harm to your marriage than good.

Remember, nothing flourishes on its own—not even a beautiful and peaceful home. You must be intentional from the beginning. Don't wait until problems arise before seeking help or learning how to improve your marriage.

Most importantly, do not go through this journey alone—carry your spouse along in the process of learning, unlearning, and relearning the things that will make your marriage beautiful.

Thank you, and may God bless your home!

OUR STORY

I want to share our wedding story with you, hoping that you and your partner can learn a lesson or two from our experience. We had our introduction ceremony on January 31, 2014, which was also the day we set our wedding date—May 16, 2015.

Our wedding was solely sponsored by my husband, my mother, my mother-in-law, and me. None of us had to go into debt, even though we didn't have much, and the day turned out beautifully. What made this possible was the strategy we used.

From the start, my husband and I agreed to have a wedding within our budget without going into debt because we weren't trying to impress anyone. We believed that our wedding didn't need to be the grandest or most extravagant since it was just one day. Instead, we were committed to building a marriage that would serve as a positive example for others. By God's grace, that's exactly what happened and continues to happen. Our prayers were answered. So, it's essential to decide what matters more to you—the wedding day or the marriage itself.

After choosing the date, the four of us decided to work together as a team. We listed the most important items needed for the day and began purchasing them one by one. It didn't matter who spent more or less; what mattered was that we set monthly targets to meet our goals.

My mother and I even removed some traditional items from the bride's family list and reduced others. Thankfully, I was able to convince her that those things wouldn't determine the success of the marriage.

We paid all our vendors before the wedding day. Unlike some who budget based on anticipated gifts, we didn't rely on monetary gifts from guests to cover any expenses.

For our pre-wedding photoshoot, we kept it simple, wearing just shirts and jeans—nothing extravagant. Interestingly, I purchased my wedding dress three months before the wedding. Our gradual, strategic buying approach saved us from unnecessary stress.

LESSONS LEARNED

Despite our careful planning, I learned some valuable lessons from a few mistakes along the way:

1. Changing My Hairstylist

Before my wedding, I had a stylist I always used when visiting my hometown. She understood my hair well and knew which styles suited me best. However, I decided to switch to a different stylist for the wedding, thinking I needed someone "special" for the big day.

This turned out to be a mistake. The new stylist charged more, didn't execute the style as I wanted, and arrived late. I was disappointed and self-conscious about my hairstyle on the way to the church, which affected my mood. In hindsight, I should have stuck with the person who knew my hair best.

2. Makeup Issues

I wanted a simple yet beautiful look. The makeup artist I chose did an excellent job for my introduction ceremony, which is why my husband and I decided to use the same person again for the wedding. However, the wedding makeup didn't turn out as well as I had hoped, possibly because she arrived late.

3. Not Sleeping Enough

Celebrations can be exhausting, especially when you're the host. I was so focused on ensuring everything was perfect for our guests that I neglected my well-being. As a result, I didn't get enough sleep the night before.

Adding to this, my period unexpectedly started the night before the wedding, likely due to stress. I had to search for sanitary pads late at night because I wasn't at home. In hindsight, I should have heeded my mother's advice to rest and let others handle the final details.

4. Forgetting to Eat

It's common to hear that celebrants don't eat until all guests are served, but this isn't practical. I almost did the same until my husband insisted I eat in the car before arriving at the reception. I was exhausted and hungry, and eating gave me the energy to enjoy the day.

5. Not Re-checking the Wedding Dress

After buying my wedding dress, I kept it hidden, even from my mother, who accompanied me to purchase it, because I wanted it to be a surprise. Unfortunately, I didn't try it on again a week before the wedding.

My husband and I had completed a 30-day fast shortly before our wedding, and I lost some weight as a result. On the wedding day, the dress was loose. We scrambled to find a needle and thread for last-minute adjustments, which added unnecessary stress.

6. Letting Little Things Affect My Mood

My hairstyle, makeup, ill-fitting dress, unexpected period, and fatigue combined to sour my mood. I wasn't smiling in the early wedding photos until my husband reminded me to focus on the joy of the day and our new life together. His words helped me shift my mindset, allowing me to genuinely smile in the rest of the pictures.

Looking back, I'm grateful for that reminder because those pictures captured memories I'll cherish forever.

This was the first outfit for our pre-wedding pictures.

This was the second outfit. I'm sure you'll agree it doesn't look like your typical pre-wedding attire — but we rocked it, unbothered by what anyone might say.

This picture was taken during our introduction ceremony. This is the makeup I was referring to — simple, yet beautiful.

This picture was taken at a time when I was still caught up in everything that hadn't gone the way I envisioned. Looking at my expression, I can't imagine not having another photo to capture the memory of that day. Thankfully, my husband reminded me to focus on us—not on everything else—and that made all the difference, as you'll see next.

I'm sure you can spot the difference between this and the previous picture. I'm grateful I listened to my husband—this has remained my favorite wedding photo.

FINAL THOUGHTS

I hope our story has given you some insights and helpful lessons for your wedding planning. It's easy to get caught up in the details, but always remember to focus on the bigger picture—building a happy and enduring marriage.

May your wedding day be beautiful and memorable, and may your marriage be blessed and fulfilling in Jesus' name, Amen

Connect with the writer, **Aderonke Samuel**

A Relationship Coach

Facebook: Aderonke Samuel

Instagram: Aderonke Samuel/thedoingcouple

YouTube Page: TheDoingCouple

www.ingramcontent.com/pod-product-compliance
Lightning Source LLC
Chambersburg PA
CBHW030050100426
42734CB00038B/994